2 Limit 2 Books per Subject
During School Year

THE *New Hampshire* COLONY

Our Thirteen Colonies

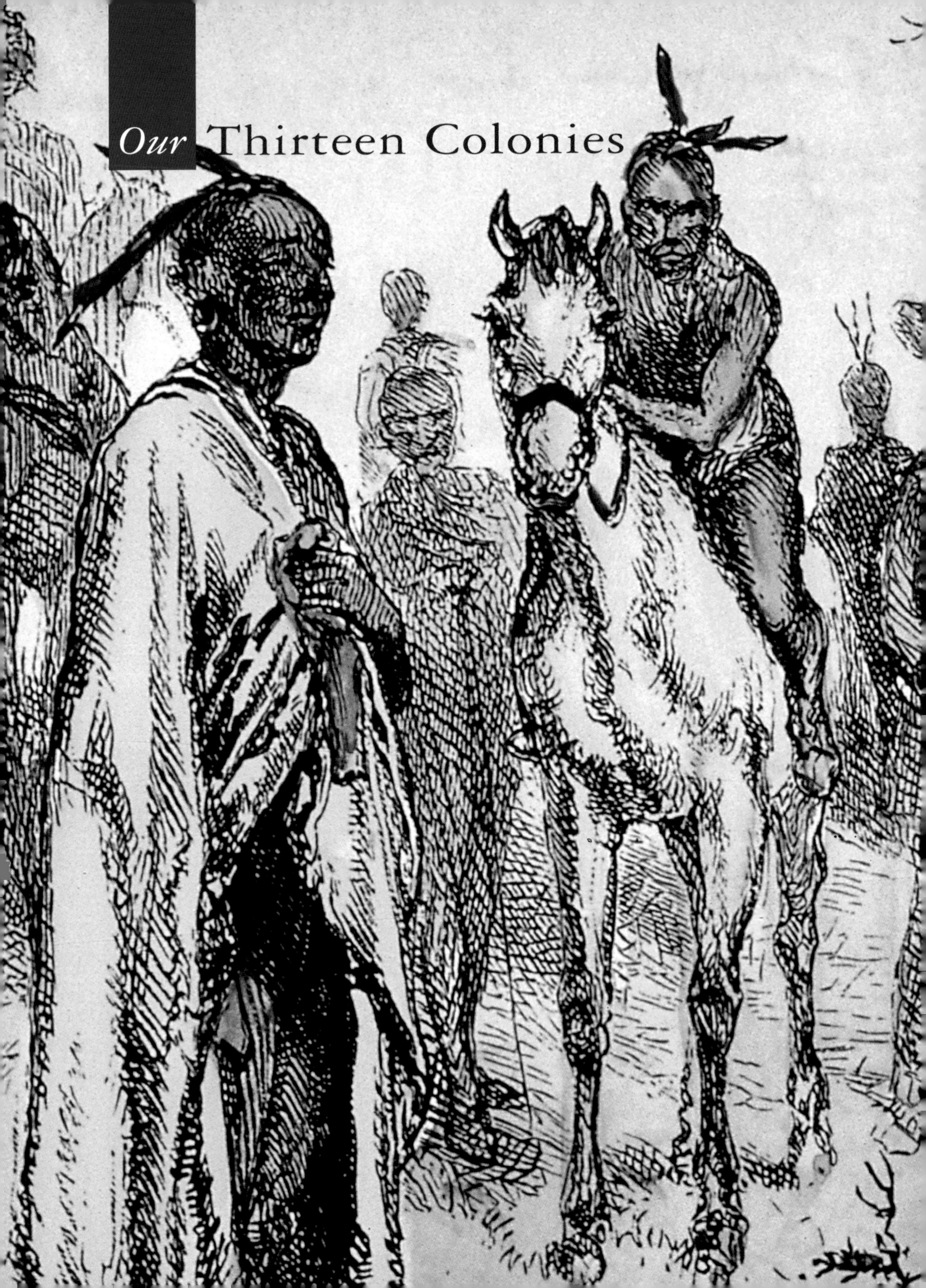

SPIRIT
of America®

THE *New Hampshire* COLONY

By Kevin Davis

Content Adviser: Marla Miller, Ph.D. Director, Public History Program,
University of Massachusetts, Amherst, Massachusetts

The Child's World®

The Child's World®
Chanhassen, Minnesota

8

THE *New Hampshire* COLONY

Published in the United States of America by The Child's World®
PO Box 326 • Chanhassen, MN 55317-0326 • 800-599-READ • www.childsworld.com

Acknowledgments
The Child's World®: Mary Berendes, Publishing Director

Editorial Directions, Inc.: E. Russell Primm, Editorial Director; Melissa McDaniel, Line Editor; Elizabeth K. Martin, Assistant Editor; Olivia Nellums, Editorial Assistant; Susan Hindman, Copy Editor; Joanne Mattern, Proofreader; Kevin Cunningham, Peter Garnham, Ruthanne Swiatkowski, Fact Checkers; Tim Griffin/IndexServ, Indexer; Cian Loughlin O'Day, Photo Researcher; Linda S. Koutris, Photo Selector

Photo
Cover: North Wind Picture Archives; Bettmann/Corbis: 12, 18, 19, 21, 33; Corbis: 6 (David Muench); 8 (The Mariner's Museum), 9 (Phil Schermeister), 13 (Gianni Dagli Orti), 14 (Ric Ergenbright), 23 (Kevin Fleming), 24, 28 (Emanuel Gottlieb Leutze), 35 (Lee Snider; Lee Snider); Getty Images/Hulton Archive: 10, 15, 16, 17, 22, 29, 32, 34; North Wind Picture Archives: 11, 20, 25, 27, 30; Stock Montage: 26.

Library of Congress Cataloging-in-Publication Data
Davis, Kevin (Kevin A.)
  The New Hampshire colony / by Kevin Davis.
    p. cm. — (Our colonies)
"Spirit of America."
Summary: Traces the history of New Hampshire, discussing the daily life of Indian tribes before the seventeenth century, European exploration and settlement, the Indian wars, colonial life, the Revolutionary War, and ratification as the ninth state. Includes bibliographical references (p.) and index.
  ISBN 1-56766-617-5 (alk. paper)
  1. New Hampshire—History—Colonial period, ca. 1600–1775—Juvenile literature. 2. New Hampshire—History—1775–1865—Juvenile literature. [1. New Hampshire—History—Colonial period, ca. 1600–1775. 2. New Hampshire—History—1775–1865.] I. Title. II. Series.
  F37.D34 2003   2003003771

Contents

Chapter ONE

The Native Americans of New Hampshire

The thick forests of New Hampshire were home to many Algonquian-speaking Native Americans before the Europeans arrived.

NATIVE AMERICANS HAD LIVED IN NORTH America for many thousands of years before the first European explorers arrived. New Hampshire was home to about 5,000 native people when Europeans first got there in the early 1600s.

The Native Americans of New Hampshire lived in villages in a beautiful land covered with thick forests, mountains, lakes, rivers, and streams. Most belonged to the Algonquian language family. People who

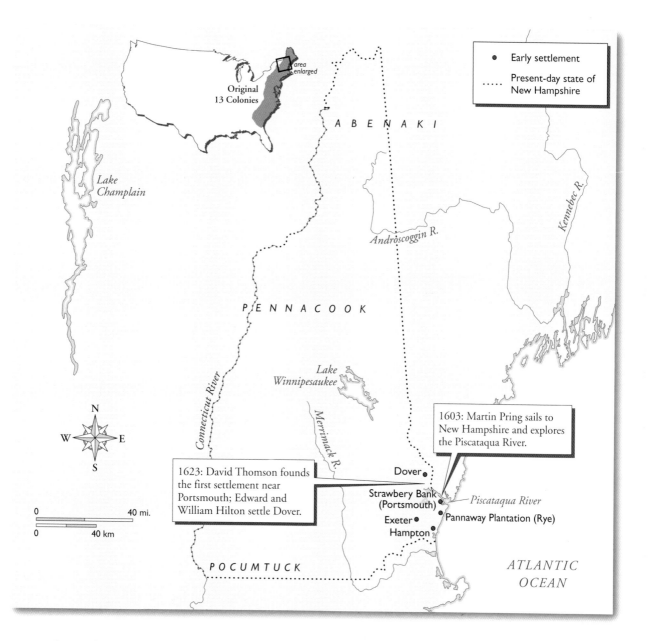

Original 13 Colonies

area enlarged

Early settlement

Present-day state of New Hampshire

A B E N A K I

Lake Champlain

Kennebec R.

Androscoggin R.

P E N N A C O O K

Lake Winnipesaukee

Connecticut River

Merrimack R.

N
W E
S

1603: Martin Pring sails to New Hampshire and explores the Piscataqua River.

1623: David Thomson founds the first settlement near Portsmouth; Edward and William Hilton settle Dover.

Dover

Strawbery Bank (Portsmouth)

Piscataqua River

Pannaway Plantation (Rye)

Exeter

Hampton

0   40 mi.
0   40 km

P O C U M T U C K

ATLANTIC OCEAN

New Hampshire Colony at the time of the first European settlement

spoke Algonquian languages were spread over the eastern seaboard, from Canada to North Carolina. Several different groups lived in eastern New Hampshire, including the Ossipees and Pequawkets. Farther inland were the

7

Light canoes were essential to survival for the Algonquians, who relied on them for both transport and fishing.

were the Pennacooks and the Piscataquas.

New Hampshire's native people lived in dome-shaped homes called wigwams. These were frameworks of wooden poles covered with bark or animal skins. The people moved at different times of the year. Sometimes they would move to a new spot to be near good hunting or fishing areas. They would move and clear new land for farms. They would also move to more protected areas when the weather got colder.

The Native Americans of New Hampshire hunted, fished, and trapped animals to survive. The men hunted deer, moose, turkey, and bears with spears and arrows. They also fished in New Hampshire's lakes and rivers, using canoes made from hollowed-out trees. The women did most of the farming. Their main crops were corn, beans, squash, and pumpkins. They also collected wild fruits and berries.

They cooked stews made from meat and vegetables. They made maple syrup and sugar from the sap of maple trees. The women preserved food by smoking it or, in the winter, packing it in snow.

Native American children did not have schools as we know them today. They were taught to hunt, farm, and fish by their parents and **elders,** and they helped with daily chores.

The Native Americans of New Hampshire had great respect for nature. They believed in many spirits and gods for the rivers, mountains, lakes, and forests. They held festivals to celebrate harvests and other important events. For fun, they made music with drums and flutes. They also sang, danced, and told stories.

Interesting Fact

▶ Like other Native American tribes in New Hampshire, the Abenaki had a great respect for nature. Although they hunted many animals, they refused to kill crows because they believed the birds brought them the corn they grew.

The many different groups of Native Americans living in New Hampshire all depended on maize, or wild corn, for food. Until they were introduced to maize by these native people, Europeans had used the word "corn" to refer to barley and wheat.

9

▶ Historians estimate that diseases introduced by Europeans killed 95 percent of New Hampshire's Native American population before most settlers arrived.

Trade with the Europeans proved deadly for the Native Americans and their way of life.

The Native American way of life began changing as soon as European explorers arrived in the Americas. One reason was that the Europeans brought diseases such as measles and smallpox, which were new to North America. Because the Native Americans had never before been exposed to these diseases, their bodies could not fight them. Many Native Americans in New Hampshire died from these diseases, and millions died across North America.

ONE OF THE GREAT NATIVE AMERICAN leaders during the early colonial period was Passaconaway, of the Pennacook tribe. In the early and mid-1600s, he ruled over a large part of **New England** that included New Hampshire. He worked hard to keep peace with the English settlers.

Passaconaway was known as the great sachem, which in Algonquian meant "chief." He was a man of great physical skill and was believed to have magical powers. Native Americans thought that Passaconaway had the ability to make water run and trees dance and that he could turn himself into a flame. They also believed he could make dry leaves in winter turn green and make the skin of a dead snake turn into a live snake.

Passaconaway became chief sometime around 1620. By this time, his people had been devastated by the diseases brought to North America by European settlers. In 1660, as he prepared to give up his leadership, Passaconaway invited English settlers to a huge feast. He felt it was important to work with the settlers. He told other Native Americans that fighting the settlers would be useless. He said he did not have the power to overcome them. The Pennacook people say that Passaconaway lived to be 100 years old. New Hampshire's Mount Passaconaway is named after the great chief.

Chapter TWO

A Colony's Beginnings

New Hampshire's forest-lands supplied much of the lumber necessary to build England's huge fleet of sea-going vessels, which included ships for both its navy and for trade.

IN THE EARLY 1600S, EUROPEAN RULERS AND wealthy businessmen began to send explorers to North America, hoping to take advantage of the natural resources there. Ships sailed to the northeast coast for its excellent fishing.

Most of the rivers in New Hampshire were too wild for ships to sail up. But the falls and rapids on these rivers could be used to power sawmills. England was also interested in the tall white pines, which they used to make the masts on their ships.

One Englishman who visited what is now New

Hampshire was Martin Pring. He was hired by merchants to find a shortcut to Asia and to bring back sassafras tree roots, which were believed to cure many illnesses. In 1603, Pring and his crew arrived at the coast on two ships called *Speedwell* and *Discoverer.* They sailed into the Piscataqua River.

King James I founded the Council for New England, whose job it was to create new settlements in North America.

They didn't find any sassafras or a shortcut to Asia. They decided to go back to England.

England sent others to explore the east coast of America. In 1607, a group led by John Smith established the first permanent English settlement in America in Jamestown, Virginia. King James I of England liked the idea of building more settlements in this new land. In

13

1620, he created the Council for New England. The council would grant land to people and oversee the development of colonies.

In 1622, the council granted 6,000 acres (2,430 hectares) of land to David Thomson to establish a fishing colony in New Hampshire. In 1623, Thomson and his crew built a small settlement near the ocean called Pannaway Plantation. The settlement included a large house, workshops, a fort, and racks for salt-drying fish. Pannaway Plantation was where the town of Rye now sits.

The Council for New England also granted a large area of land from the Kennebec River to the Merrimack River to Captain John Mason and Sir Ferdinando Gorges in 1622. They later divided the land.

Large ships couldn't venture down the wild rivers of New England. But the rocky coastline of what is now Rye, New Hampshire, shown here, provided a good location for a community based on fishing.

14

Gorges got an area that became the colony of Maine, and Mason got an area between the Merrimack and Piscataqua Rivers. Mason, who was from Hampshire County in England, named the area New Hampshire. Though he remained in England, he sent colonists to New Hampshire to create a settlement called Strawbery Banke, which got its name from the wild strawberries that grew there. The settlement eventually grew into the town of Portsmouth. Even though Mason was granted the land, he never visited New Hampshire.

Other settlers came to New Hampshire and built towns along the coast. Edward and William Hilton came to New Hampshire and established a settlement called Dover.

Early settlers arrive at Odiorne's Point, the New Hampshire site where Pannaway Plantation was established. David Thomson's son John was the first English child born in New Hampshire.

Early colonial life was often harsh and difficult. Because the early settlers of New Hampshire lived off the land, they had to do their own farming and building and make their own goods. Women played a vital role in this. They made soap and candles, spun yarn and wove cloth to make clothing, preserved and baked food, and took care of their families.

New Hampshire grew more slowly than some of the other colonies because the land was demanding and the winters were very cold. By 1640, there were only about 1,000 settlers in New Hampshire in four main towns: Dover, Strawbery Banke (Portsmouth), Exeter, and Hampton.

Colonial farms and households could not have functioned without the long hours put in by women, who were responsible for many tedious and time-consuming tasks.

FOR THE FIRST 50 YEARS AFTER EUROPEANS SETTLED IN NEW HAMPSHIRE, they generally got along with the Native Americans in the area. The native people taught the settlers about planting corn, beans, and pumpkins. They showed settlers how to make dishes, such as succotash, from cooked corn and beans. But as more European settlers arrived, tensions increased. As Native Americans lost more and more land to the Europeans, these tensions turned into wars.

In 1689, a group of Native Americans attacked a settlement at Dover, beginning what is called King William's War. This war lasted until 1697. Another war, called Queen Anne's War, lasted from 1702 until 1713. During these wars, native people raided white settlements, and white people burned native villages and crops. Hundreds of people were killed on both sides. The colonists attacked more Native American villages in the 1720s. After that, most Native Americans left New Hampshire. They had been forced to abandon the land where their families had lived for hundreds of years.

Chapter THREE

The Growing Colony

Like many of the early settlements, the Massachusetts Bay Colony expected all the colonists to strictly follow the rules of their religion.

THE SETTLERS OF NEW HAMPSHIRE AND THE other colonies lived independent lives. But they were still subject to control by the king of England and the English **Parliament,** which wanted to make money from the land.

For much of its early history, New Hampshire was not a separate colony. Instead, it was under the control of the Massachusetts Bay Colony, based in Boston. The Massachusetts Bay Colony was the center of New England during the early colonial period. It governed an area from

Cape Cod to Maine. Many colonists were not happy because Massachusetts made rules about trade and religious freedom in New Hampshire.

In 1679, King Charles II made New Hampshire a separate royal colony. This meant that the colony was directly under the king's control. The king chose John Cutt, a merchant in Portsmouth, to be New Hampshire's president. The king also appointed a council to oversee the colony. The people of New Hampshire had control of their towns and had small **assemblies,** but England still had the final say in all matters. In 1686, King James II got rid of the assemblies and created a single unit called the Dominion of New England to oversee New Hampshire, Massachusetts, Rhode Island, and Connecticut—and, later, New York and New Jersey.

King James II ended the self-government of New Hampshire and other colonies with the creation of the Dominion of New England.

Royal Governor Benning Wentworth was an important force in New Hampshire gaining its independence from the Massachusetts Bay Colony.

It wasn't until 1741 that New Hampshire was independent again. Benning Wentworth became royal governor of the colony. He held the post of governor from 1741 to 1767—longer than anyone else. His nephew, John Wentworth, took over and served until 1775. The Wentworths were very popular with the people of New Hampshire.

During the early 1700s, many more people came to New Hampshire. Some of them were African slaves. Slavery was not as common in New Hampshire as in the southern colonies. But a small number of enslaved people worked as house servants or farm laborers. Others worked as carpenters, blacksmiths, or bakers. Most slaves lived in and around Portsmouth. New Hampshire had an estimated 633 slaves in 1767, but by 1775, there were only 479.

In 1767, New Hampshire had more than 140 towns with about 52,700 settlers. New Hampshire's most important town was Portsmouth, which was the capital of New Hampshire until 1808. It was a thriving city of merchants, sailors, traders, and wealthy businessmen.

Hundreds of ships sailed from Portsmouth to the waters off the New Hampshire coast to fish for pollock and cod. Most of the fish was dried and sent back to England. Ships that operated out of Portsmouth also carried lumber, oil, and livestock. Large pine logs from New Hampshire's forests were sent

The charter for Dartmouth was granted by King George III in 1769, when the college moved from Connecticut to New Hampshire.

21

During the 1700s, Portsmouth's shipbuilding industry increased dramatically. Ships made from the extremely hard woods available nearby could withstand the battering of strong waves as well as the battering they received in battle.

to England to make ship masts. Many ships also sailed from Portsmouth to the British islands in the Caribbean Sea. After they were unloaded, the ships were filled with products from the islands, including sugar and rum. Other ships arrived in Portsmouth from England with manufactured goods such as glass, china, furniture, tools, and books.

Colonists in Portsmouth also traded with the Native Americans for beaver furs, which were very popular in England for hats and coats. In return, they gave the native people blankets, guns, knives, and glass beads.

Shipbuilding also became a big business in Portsmouth. New Hampshire shipbuilders built many ships for the British navy. But they also built many ships that were used during the Revolutionary War to fight against the British.

THE TOWN OF LONDONDERRY WAS SETTLED BY A GROUP OF PEOPLE WHO came to America from Ireland. These families had originally been from Scotland, so they were known as Scotch-Irish. They had moved to Ireland because they wanted the freedom to practice their Presbyterian faith. They were not happy in Ireland either. They were forced to pay taxes to support the Church of England and were not allowed to own land.

A group of Scotch-Irish sold most of their belongings and sailed in five ships to America, landing in Boston in 1718. In 1722, the new town of Londonderry, New Hampshire, was founded. Soon, other Scotch-Irish began coming to this new community.

The Scotch-Irish who came to Londonderry were educated crafts-people. They introduced the production of high-quality linen to America. Linen cloth is made from flax, a plant they had brought with them from Ireland. Londonderry linen was considered the best in New England. Presidents George Washington and Thomas Jefferson were said to have worn Londonderry linen.

Chapter FOUR

During the War

George Washington, serving as a major under the British, led many colonists into battle during the French and Indian War.

DURING THE 1600S AND 1700S, BRITAIN AND France competed for control of North America. In 1754, this competition turned into the French and Indian War. By 1763, Britain had defeated France, gaining control of all land east of the Mississippi River. But the war left Great Britain heavily in debt. The British tried to raise money to pay off their debts by taxing the colonies.

Many colonists were unhappy with British rules and taxes. Like people in the other colonies, many in New Hampshire wanted to be

24

independent. They felt that they should have more say in governing their own affairs.

Throughout New England, anti-British feeling grew. Colonists protested laws such as the Stamp Act, which required that colo-

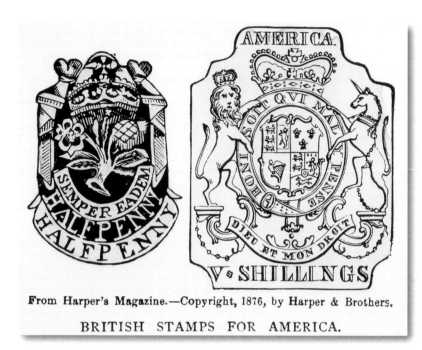

From Harper's Magazine.—Copyright, 1876, by Harper & Brothers.

BRITISH STAMPS FOR AMERICA.

nists pay taxes on all documents and newspapers. The British ended the Stamp Act, but then passed taxes on other goods. Again the colonists protested. Women did their part by refusing to buy English products such as tea and cloth. On December 16, 1773, a group of men from Massachusetts got on British ships at Boston Harbor and dumped chests of tea into the water to protest the tax on tea. This event became known as the Boston Tea Party.

The people of New Hampshire were not involved in many of the early protests in New England. For the most part, they were well-off.

Under the Stamp Act, colonists were required to pay fees for nearly every piece of paper they used, as well as many other goods that were a part of daily life.

First Continental Congress representative John Sullivan was also responsible for organizing the raid on Fort William and Mary. In the following years, he helped the Patriot cause in other important ways as well.

Interesting Fact

▶ When the New Hampshire colonists turned against the British, their governor fled. But his three military regiments sided with the Patriots.

But hearing about the protests in other colonies inspired New Hampshire colonists to support the coming revolution.

The First **Continental Congress** met in 1774 to discuss the problems with Britain. Representatives from all the colonies except Georgia went to Philadelphia. John Sullivan and Nathaniel Folsom represented New Hampshire.

Britain did not want to lose control of the colonies, and British soldiers began to prepare for war. Paul Revere, a colonist from Boston, rode into Portsmouth to warn that British troops were coming to guard Fort William and Mary at New Castle. On December 14, 1774, several hundred New Hampshire **Patriots** raided the fort and took guns, cannons, and gunpowder. It was one of the first major acts of rebellion that led to the revolution.

26

In May 1775, the Second Continental Congress met. New Hampshire sent John Sullivan and John Langdon to represent the colony. The Continental Congress elected George Washington to lead the Continental army. The Congress also called on colonies to form their own states.

No battles were fought in New Hampshire during the Revolutionary War. But many soldiers from New Hampshire fought in the war, including about 180 African-Americans. One of them was a former slave named Prince Whipple. He was an assistant to General George Washington. He is believed to be the African-American portrayed in a famous painting of Washington crossing the Delaware River.

In January 1776, New Hampshire became the first colony to establish its own government outside English rule. In

New Hampshire sent many brave Patriots into battle against the British, but none of those battles were fought in their home state.

In the famous painting Washington Crossing the Delaware, *the man circled here is thought to be Whipple. Experts believe that as many as 180 black New Hampshire men fought in the Revolutionary War.*

Philadelphia, Thomas Jefferson wrote the Declaration of Independence, which was approved on July 4, 1776. Josiah Bartlett, Matthew Thornton, and William Whipple of New Hampshire signed the declaration.

But the war was far from over. The colonists got a much-needed boost when France sent troops to help the Americans. The British finally gave up after a major battle at Yorktown, Virginia. The war officially ended on September 3, 1783, when the Americans signed a peace **treaty** with Great Britain in Paris, France.

TWO IMPORTANT MILITARY LEADERS IN THE REVOLUTIONARY WAR CAME FROM New Hampshire. They were Major General John Sullivan and Major General John Stark.

Sullivan was born in Somersworth, New Hampshire, in 1740. As a young man, Sullivan worked as a lawyer. In 1772, he was appointed major of the New Hampshire **militia.** In 1774, he was chosen to represent New Hampshire at the First Continental Congress. Sullivan led troops in the raid at Fort William and Mary, which was controlled by the British. He became a general under George Washington in 1775, and he helped Washington in many battles in Massachusetts and New Jersey.

John Stark (right) was born in Londonderry, New Hampshire, in 1728. He was a brave soldier who fought in the French and Indian War. During the Revolution, he led troops at the Battle of Bunker Hill in 1775. He also led 2,000 soldiers to victory at the Battle of Bennington at the border of Vermont and New York in 1777. Stark was famous for his words, "Live free or die," which later became the state motto.

Chapter FIVE

Becoming a Nation

Citizens of Portsmouth shared in the pride that the Patriots felt in their victory over the British. But many difficulties had to be overcome before the city was once again the prosperous, growing place it had been before the war.

WHEN THE REVOLUTIONARY WAR ENDED, there was a great celebration in Portsmouth. It began with the firing of 13 guns at six o'clock in the morning. Throughout the day and into the night, there were feasts, fireworks, and a grand ball.

But the war had been won at great cost to New Hampshire. Thousands of men were killed. Their families were in debt. Portsmouth lost much of its shipping business. The people had to rebuild the economy. Soldiers

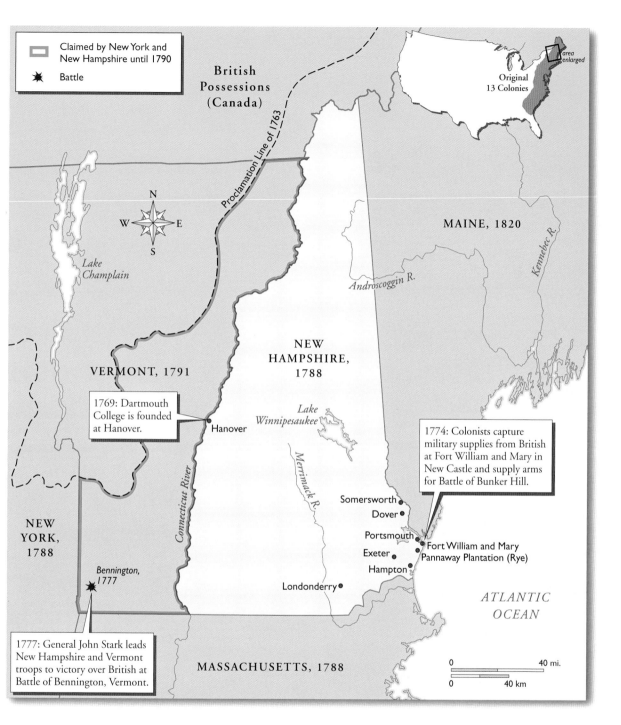

British
Possessions
(Canada)

Original
13 Colonies

area
enlarged

Proclamation Line of 1763

N
W   E
S

MAINE, 1820

Lake
Champlain

Androscoggin R.

Kennebec R.

NEW
HAMPSHIRE,
1788

VERMONT, 1791

1769: Dartmouth
College is founded
at Hanover.

Hanover

Lake
Winnipesaukee

1774: Colonists capture
military supplies from British
at Fort William and Mary in
New Castle and supply arms
for Battle of Bunker Hill.

Merrimack R.

Somersworth
Dover

NEW
YORK,
1788

Portsmouth
Exeter
Hampton

Fort William and Mary
Pannaway Plantation (Rye)

Connecticut River

Bennington,
1777

Londonderry

ATLANTIC
OCEAN

1777: General John Stark leads
New Hampshire and Vermont
troops to victory over British at
Battle of Bennington, Vermont.

MASSACHUSETTS, 1788

0   40 mi.

0   40 km

returned to their farms and tried to make a
living. Settlers moved farther inland, and
towns eventually started to grow again.

*New Hampshire Colony
before statehood*

31

From the beginning, John Langdon strongly favored revolution, and his contributions in bringing the new country into being were many. Throughout most of his life he remained actively involved in politics.

Once the colonies declared their independence from Great Britain, they had to set about creating their own government and organizing themselves into a country. First, the Continental Congress created the **Articles of Confederation,** which outlined an agreement establishing the new country. It was approved in 1781, but it provided for a very weak national government. The new government could not impose taxes and did not have a president or a national court system.

Some colonial leaders wanted a strong central government. In 1787, representatives met in Philadelphia to create a new **constitution.** John Langdon and Nicholas Gilman came from New Hampshire. The representatives all worked together to write new laws to govern the land. Nine of the

13 states had to approve the new Constitution before it could become law.

The people of New Hampshire were at first unsure about approving the new U.S. Constitution. They were proud of their independence. Representatives in New Hampshire argued against a strong central government. They did not believe that a larger government that was based far away could do a better job than their own government at home.

Much brilliant thought went into the wording of the U.S. Constitution. Its principles have remained the strong guiding force throughout America's history.

On June 21, 1788, the representatives from New Hampshire finally agreed to vote in favor of the U.S. Constitution. New Hampshire was the ninth state to approve the Constitution. Other states were still hesitant to approve it. Many were won over by the promise that a **Bill of Rights** would be added to the Constitution, guaranteeing individual rights such as freedom of religion.

Portsmouth soon held another great celebration. The new president, George Washington, came to visit. The city honored the man known as the father of the country with three days of parades, music, and fireworks.

After the United States was born, John Langdon became the first acting vice president of the new country. He later became president

There was a great celebration when George Washington visited Portsmouth after New Hampshire accepted the new Constitution. The creation of that important document officially marked America's adoption of a new form of government.

of the U.S. Senate when George Washington was elected president.

Even though New Hampshire was one of the smallest colonies, its people made great contributions and sacrifices to help create the United States of America. The state motto, "Live Free or Die," sums up their independent spirit.

New Hampshire's state motto, "Live Free or Die," was written by General John Stark and captures one of the important ideas upheld by democratic societies throughout the world.

1603   Englishman Martin Pring sails to New Hampshire and explores the Piscataqua River.

1622   The Council for New England grants Sir Ferdinando Gorges and Captain John Mason land between the Merrimack and Kennebec Rivers. David Thomson founds New Hampshire's first settlement near Portsmouth. Edward and William Hilton settle Dover.

1629   John Mason receives the area between the Merrimack and Piscataqua Rivers, which he names New Hampshire.

1633   The first church in New Hampshire is established in Dover.

1641   New Hampshire is placed under the government of the Massachusetts Bay Colony.

1679   New Hampshire becomes a royal colony.

1686   New Hampshire is made part of the Dominion of New England.

1692   New Hampshire becomes a separate colony.

1741   Benning Wentworth becomes governor of New Hampshire.

1763   Great Britain defeats France in the French and Indian War.

1767   John Wentworth becomes governor of New Hampshire.

1769   Dartmouth College is founded in Hanover.

1774   Colonists capture military supplies from the British at Fort William and Mary in New Castle.

1775   The American Revolution begins. Governor John Wentworth flees Portsmouth.

1776   The Declaration of Independence is signed.

1777   General John Stark leads New Hampshire and Vermont troops to victory over the British at the Battle of Bennington.

1784   The New Hampshire state constitution is adopted.

1788   New Hampshire becomes the ninth state to approve the U.S. Constitution.

Glossary TERMS

Articles of Confederation (AR-tuh-kuhls uv kon-fed-uh-RAY-shun)
The Articles of Confederation was the first constitution of the United States. It was replaced by the U.S. Constitution in 1788.

assemblies (uh-SEM-blees)
Assemblies are groups of people who get together to make rules and laws. The people of New Hampshire had small assemblies to govern their towns.

Bill of Rights (BILL uv RITES)
The Bill of Rights is a list of individual rights that are protected, such as freedom of speech and freedom of religion. The Bill of Rights is the first 10 amendments, or changes, to the U.S. Constitution.

constitution (kon-stuh-TOO-shun)
A constitution is a document outlining the structure and basic laws of a government. New Hampshire was the first colony to write its own constitution.

Continental Congress (kon-tuh-NENT-uhl KON-griss)
The Continental Congress was a meeting of colonists that served as the American government during Revolutionary times. The Second Continental Congress adopted the Declaration of Independence in 1776.

elders (EL-duhrs)
Elders are older, experienced people. Native American children were taught to hunt, farm, and fish by their elders.

militia (mill-ISH-uh)
A militia is a local, part-time army. New Hampshire had several militias that helped battle the British during the Revolutionary War.

New England (NOO ING-luhnd)
New England is the northeastern part of the United States. New Hampshire is one of the six New England states.

Parliament (PAR-luh-muhnt)
Parliament is the lawmaking body of Great Britain. After the French and Indian War, Parliament began passing taxes on the American colonies.

Patriots (PAY-tree-uhts)
Patriots were colonists who supported independence from Britain. Many Patriots from New Hampshire fought in the Revolutionary War.

treaty (TREE-tee)
A treaty is an agreement. Americans signed a peace treaty with Great Britain in 1783, officially ending the Revolutionary War.

Josiah Bartlett (1729–1795)

Continental Congress delegate, 1775–76, 1778–79; Declaration of Independence signer; Articles of Confederation signer; New Hampshire superior court associate justice, 1782–88; New Hampshire superior court chief justice, 1788–90; Constitutional Convention delegate, 1787; New Hampshire president, 1790–92; New Hampshire governor, 1793–94

Nicholas Gilman (1755–1814)

Continental Congress delegate, 1787–89; Constitutional Convention delegate, 1787; U.S. Constitution signer; U.S. Representative member, 1789–97; U.S. senator, 1805–14

John Langdon (1741–1819)

Continental Congress delegate, 1775–76, 1783–84; New Hampshire president, 1785–1786, 1788–89; Constitutional Convention delegate, 1787; U.S. Constitution signer; U.S. senator, 1789–1801; U.S. Senate president pro-tempore, 1789; New Hampshire governor, 1805–09, 1810–12

Matthew Thornton (1714?–1803)

New Hampshire House of Representatives president, 1776; Continental Congress delegate, 1776; Declaration of Independence signer

John Wentworth Jr. (1745–1787)

New Hampshire House of Representatives member, 1776; New Hampshire state supreme court justice, 1776–81; Articles of Confederation signer; Continental Congress delegate, 1778; New Hampshire state senator, 1784–86

William Whipple (1730–1785)

Independence signer; New Hampshire superior court associate justice, 1782–85

For Further INFORMATION

Web Sites

Visit our homepage for lots of links about the New Hampshire colony:
http://www.childsworld.com/links.html

Note to Parents, Teachers, and Librarians:
We routinely verify our Web links to make sure they're safe,
active sites—so encourage your readers to check them out!

Books

Otfinoski, Steven. *New Hampshire.* Tarrytown, N.Y.: Benchmark Books, 1999.

Stein, R. Conrad. *New Hampshire.* Danbury, Conn.: Children's Press, 2000.

Thompson, Kathleen. *New Hampshire.* Austin, Tex.: Raintree/Steck Vaughn, 1996.

Places to Visit or Contact

American Independence Museum
To learn more about life in colonial New Hampshire and New Hampshire's role in the American Revolution
One Governor's Lane
Exeter, NH 03833
603/772-2622

Museum of New Hampshire History
For all kinds of information about New Hampshire history
The Hamel Center
6 Eagle Square
Concord, NH 03301-4923
603/228-6688

Strawbery Banke Museum
To learn about life in colonial New Hampshire and see costumed guides perform traditional crafts
P.O. Box 200
Portsmouth, NH 03802
603/433-1100

Index

About the Author

KEVIN DAVIS IS A MAGAZINE WRITER, AUTHOR, AND AWARD-winning former newspaper reporter. He has written eight nonfiction children's books and a book for adults. His work has appeared in many national publications and the *Encyclopaedia Britannica Medical and Health Annual*. A graduate of the University of Illinois, he lives in Chicago.